DESTINATION SPACE

VOYAGE TO PLUTO

by Liz Kruesi

FOCUS READERS

www.focusreaders.com

Focus Readers is distributed by North Star Editions:
sales@northstareditions.com | 888-417-0195

Produced for Focus Readers by Red Line Editorial.

Content Consultant: Dr. David A. Weintraub, Professor of Astronomy, Department of Physics & Astronomy, Vanderbilt University

Photographs ©: Johns Hopkins University Applied Physics Laboratory/Southwest Research Institute/JPL/NASA, cover, 1, 14, 22, 25, 26–27, 28, 33, 35, 38 (spacecraft), 42–43; Kim Shiflett/KSC/NASA, 4–5; KSC/NASA, 7, 9, 12–13; Joel Kowsky/HQ/NASA, 11; JPL/JHUAPL/NASA, 16; Bill Ingalls/NASA/AP Images, 18–19; Mark Garlick/Science Photo Library/Alamy, 21; ESA/H. Weaver JHUAPL/A. Stern SwRI/HST Pluto Companion Search Team/JPL/NASA, 30–31; edobric/Shutterstock Images, 36–37; shooarts/Shutterstock Images, 38 (Earth), 38 (Jupiter), 38 (Pluto); Johns Hopkins University Applied Physics Laboratory/Southwest Research Institute/Alex Parker/JPL/NASA, 40; JPL/NASA, 45

ISBN
978-1-63517-500-4 (hardcover)
978-1-63517-572-1 (paperback)
978-1-63517-716-9 (ebook pdf)
978-1-63517-644-5 (hosted ebook)

Library of Congress Control Number: 2017948056

Printed in the United States of America
Mankato, MN
November, 2017

ABOUT THE AUTHOR

Liz Kruesi found her love of astronomy at a young age, during family trips to the Adirondack Mountains. She studied physics and astrophysics in college and graduate school, and her writing has appeared in *Astronomy*, *Discover*, *Popular Science*, and other publications.

TABLE OF CONTENTS

CHAPTER 1
The Voyage Begins 5

PERSON OF IMPACT
Alan Stern 10

CHAPTER 2
Speedy Spacecraft 13

CHAPTER 3
Pluto Discoveries 19

FOCUS ON TECHNOLOGY
Taking Photos in Space 24

CHAPTER 4
An Amazing Atmosphere 27

CHAPTER 5
Pluto's Moons 31

CHAPTER 6
The Next Target 37

CHAPTER 7
Back to Pluto? 43

Focus on Voyage to Pluto • 46
Glossary • 47
To Learn More • 48
Index • 48

THE VOYAGE BEGINS

July 14, 2015, was an exciting day for astronomers. After traveling through space for more than nine years, the *New Horizons* **probe** had finally reached Pluto. It was the first time in history that a probe had visited the dwarf planet.

Sending a spacecraft to Pluto was not easy. Scientists first thought of a mission to Pluto in the 1960s and 1970s. They planned for the spacecraft to visit other planets along the way.

New Horizons was launched into space using an Atlas V rocket.

Scientists called the mission a Grand Tour of the solar system. The spacecraft was designed to visit Jupiter, Saturn, Uranus, Neptune, and Pluto.

However, sending a spacecraft to multiple planets proved difficult. *Voyager 1* visited Saturn in 1979 and Jupiter in 1980. Between 1979 and 1989, the *Voyager 2* spacecraft went to Jupiter, Saturn, Uranus, and Neptune. But a voyage to Pluto would have to wait.

In 1989, another group of astronomers began working on a mission to Pluto. Building and launching a spacecraft takes hundreds of millions of dollars. Every part of the spacecraft must be tested. Plus, scientists must try to anticipate potential problems. Once a spacecraft is in space, it can be difficult or even impossible to fix.

The scientists had to convince a space agency to help pay for their spacecraft. They suggested a

▲ New Horizons team members conducted a practice run of the probe's launch in 2005.

mission to Pluto many times in the 1990s. But the National Aeronautics and Space Administration (NASA) had other priorities. Finally, in 2001, NASA chose a project idea called New Horizons to move to the next phase of development. That phase involved figuring out the price, design, and schedule. The New Horizons mission was officially approved in the spring of 2003.

For the next two and a half years, scientists working on the New Horizons project were very busy. They had to make sure the expensive spacecraft could survive the long journey from Earth to Pluto. In addition, they had to test the spacecraft's cameras and other instruments. Pluto orbits the sun in the cold depths of the solar system, so scientists had to make sure the instruments would work in such chilly conditions.

On January 12, 2006, NASA deemed the New Horizons spacecraft ready to fly. The probe would travel 3.1 billion miles (4.9 billion km) to reach Pluto. At approximately 1,000 pounds (454 kg), New Horizons was relatively light for a spacecraft. But it was launched by a powerful rocket. This combination allowed the spacecraft to lift off very quickly. In fact, New Horizons had the fastest launch in history. When the probe zoomed away

⚟ A tall, curved shell called a fairing surrounded the spacecraft and protected it during launch.

from Earth on January 19, 2006, it was moving more than 36,000 miles per hour (57,900 km/h). That is more than 10 miles (16 km) per second.

ALAN STERN

Alan Stern has spent many years studying outer space. He played a key part in planning the New Horizons mission. Stern was born in 1957 in Louisiana. His love of space started when he was a child. During grade school, Stern watched the first astronauts travel to space. And in 1969, he watched as humans first walked on the moon.

In college, Stern studied physics and astronomy at the University of Texas at Austin. He attended graduate school there as well. Stern got a master's degree in aerospace engineering in 1980. The next year, he completed a second master's degree in atmospheric sciences.

Stern then worked as an engineer for six years. He helped create the instruments that go aboard spacecraft. His interest in space and flight led him to become a certified pilot. He hoped to become an astronaut, too. Stern went back to graduate

△ From 2007 to 2008, Alan Stern directed all of NASA's space and Earth science programs.

school to study planetary science. He graduated from the University of Colorado Boulder in 1989 with a PhD. That same year, he first suggested to NASA the idea of using a probe to study Pluto.

In late 2001, NASA chose Stern's mission idea. During the next four years, Stern led the team of scientists and engineers who worked on the New Horizons mission. Since then, Stern has continued to be involved in space exploration.

CHAPTER 2

SPEEDY SPACECRAFT

The *New Horizons* probe weighs 1,054 pounds (478 kg). Most of this weight comes from shielding that protects the probe's electronics from the harsh environment of space. The probe also carries fuel for its small rockets and a radioactive power source for its scientific instruments. *New Horizons* has seven scientific instruments. Together, the instruments weigh 66 pounds (30 kg).

New Horizons is approximately the size of a baby grand piano.

The instruments did many things. Cameras snapped photographs throughout the journey to Pluto. Other instruments collected data about Pluto's chemistry and environment. They recorded

➤ HOW *NEW HORIZONS* STUDIED PLUTO

PEPSSI: Measures the particles that escape from Pluto's atmosphere

SWAP: Measures the solar wind around Pluto and how Pluto interacts with it

LORRI: Uses a telescope and camera to study Pluto from a long distance and to provide detailed images of its surface

SDC: Measures the space dust that hits *New Horizons* as it travels through space

REX: Picks up radio waves sent out by giant antennas on Earth to study Pluto's atmosphere

Alice: Uses ultraviolet light to study the composition of Pluto's atmosphere and search for atmospheres around other objects

Ralph: Uses visible light and infrared light to make colored maps and thermal maps of Pluto's surface

information about the dwarf planet's **atmosphere**. An **antenna** sent this data back to Earth.

New Horizons passed Mars only three months after it launched. By June 2006, the probe had reached the **asteroid** belt between Mars and Jupiter. Millions of rocks orbit the sun in this region. Asteroids come in a variety of sizes. Most are quite small. Some are only as big as dust specks. But a few are much larger. *New Horizons* flew past one asteroid that was the size of a mountain. As the probe passed this asteroid, scientists tested one of its cameras. They also tested the technology the spacecraft used to track its target.

In February 2007, *New Horizons* flew past Jupiter. Scientists used this flyby to test the probe's scientific instruments. *New Horizons* took photos of Jupiter and its moons as well.

▲ Asteroids can be a variety of shapes and sizes.

New Horizons saw clouds form on the giant planet. The spacecraft also spent time observing Jupiter's moon Io. It even saw one of the moon's volcanoes in action. Other instruments recorded the types of chemicals in Jupiter's atmosphere. These tests helped scientists make sure the spacecraft's scientific instruments were working properly.

But NASA had another reason for flying the spacecraft so close to Jupiter. When a spacecraft swings by a planet, the spacecraft can pick up a little bit of energy from the planet. This energy boost causes the spacecraft to speed up. Flying by Jupiter gave *New Horizons* a boost of speed. The boost from the giant planet also changed the direction of the spacecraft's path. This is known as a gravitational slingshot. It set *New Horizons* on a route directly to Pluto.

A few months later, *New Horizons* fell into a deep sleep. This was all part of NASA's plan. The spacecraft had eight years of space travel left before it would reach Pluto. To conserve energy, NASA scientists woke up the probe two to three times each year. They checked its instruments to make sure there were no problems. Then they put the probe back to sleep.

Scientists woke *New Horizons* for the final time in December 2014. The probe had nearly completed its journey to Pluto.

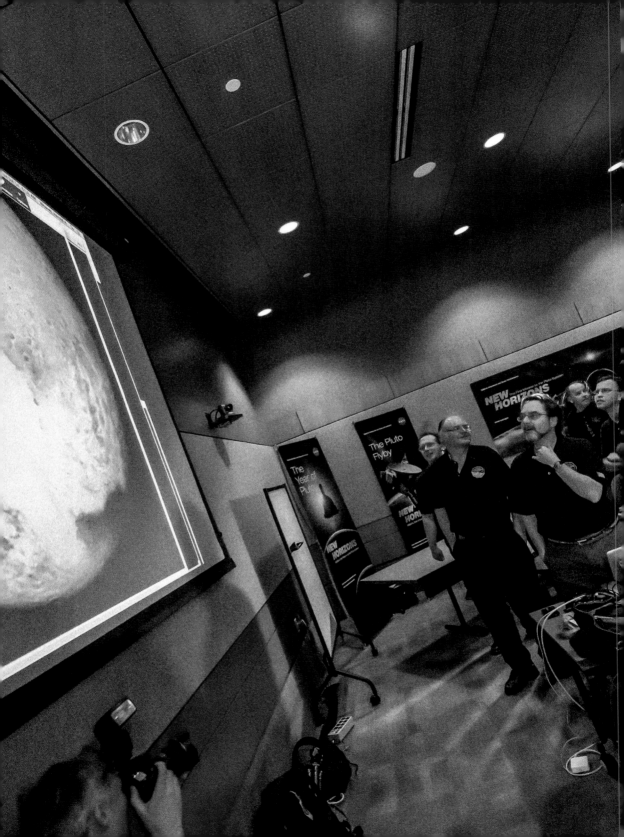

CHAPTER 3

PLUTO DISCOVERIES

The *New Horizons* spacecraft began seeing details on Pluto in the spring of 2015. But the spacecraft would not stop at Pluto. Stopping would require the spacecraft to carry more rockets and fuel. This would have made the spacecraft slower and heavier. Scientists wanted the probe to reach Pluto as quickly as possible. Therefore, they planned for *New Horizons* to fly past the dwarf planet instead of stopping.

NASA scientists view the last image *New Horizons* sent before its closest approach of Pluto.

On July 14, 2015, *New Horizons* made its closest approach to Pluto. The probe flew approximately 7,800 miles (12,500 km) above the dwarf planet. The 12-hour period before the closest approach was very busy. *New Horizons* used all its instruments to make measurements. It also took hundreds of pictures. It did the same thing during the 12 hours after the approach. A tiny antenna sent this information back to Earth.

The pictures showed scientists some surprising things about Pluto. First, Pluto's surface was younger than scientists expected. Because Pluto is small and far from the sun, scientists thought its surface would be old. Many planets with young surfaces are warm inside. These planets tend to be active. Activity on their surfaces can change their appearances. For example, the plates that make up Earth's crust sometimes rub together

△ During its closest approach, *New Horizons* was traveling 8.6 miles (14 km) per second.

and cause earthquakes. Or they can crash into one another and create mountains. And volcanoes can spew material that covers old land with new rock. Because of all this activity, the rocks on much of Earth's surface are relatively young.

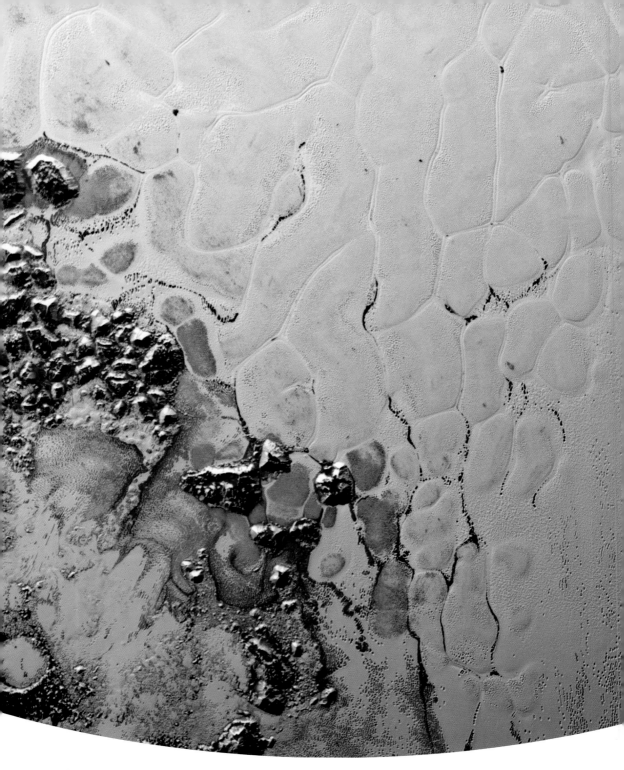

Much of Pluto's surface is made up of relatively young, smooth ice that has replaced older ice.

Scientists expected Pluto to be more like planets that are cold inside. These planets have changed very little since the solar system formed more than four billion years ago. As a result, their surfaces are covered in **craters** from asteroid and comet crashes.

Scientists were surprised to find areas on Pluto with few or no craters. One area is the size of Texas. The material in this frozen plain may be only 10 million years old. That is very young compared with the rest of the solar system.

Second, the pictures showed large amounts of water ice. The ice had recently flowed in the same way that glaciers move on Earth's surface. The pictures showed Pluto even has ice mountains that are as tall as the Appalachian Mountains in the United States. The dwarf planet may also have volcanoes that spew slush instead of hot lava.

TAKING PHOTOS IN SPACE

New Horizons uses two cameras. One camera takes only black-and-white photos. The second camera can detect many kinds of light. Its eight parts get information from one telescope. Three parts pick up black-and-white light. Other parts can detect color or **infrared** light.

On Earth, when a person takes a photo of a fast-moving car, the image is blurred. The *New Horizons* spacecraft was traveling 8.6 miles (14 km) per second when it passed Pluto. But the photos it took were not blurry. That is because the spacecraft was still very far from Pluto.

Suppose a person is flying in an airplane. She sees a mountain off in the distance. The airplane is traveling 600 miles per hour (966 km/h). That is approximately 10 miles (16 km) each minute.

△ *New Horizons* snapped many photos of Jupiter and Io, and several were compiled to create this image.

But the person is much farther than 10 miles (16 km) from the mountain. As a result, the mountain appears to stay in the same place, and she can still take an unblurred photo of it.

Compared with Earth, far less sunlight reaches Pluto. Like any spacecraft that travels far from the sun, *New Horizons* uses a special type of camera. The camera's large **aperture** lets in as much light as possible. This allows the camera to take pictures even in very low light.

CHAPTER 4

AN AMAZING ATMOSPHERE

Scientists also used *New Horizons* to study Pluto's atmosphere. The probe snapped a photo as it flew through Pluto's shadow. The photo showed how sunlight passes through the dwarf planet's atmosphere. It revealed that the atmosphere is made of multiple layers.

Pluto's atmosphere extends at least 120 miles (193 km) from the dwarf planet's surface. It is much colder and thinner than Earth's atmosphere.

More than 12 layers of haze in Pluto's atmosphere are visible over a mountain range.

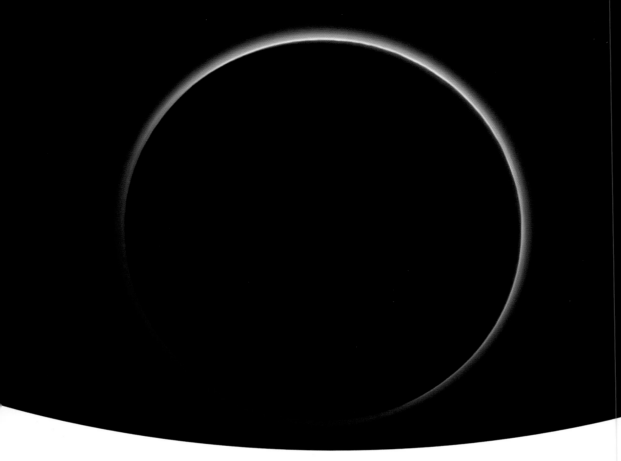

New Horizons photographed a layer of blue haze surrounding Pluto.

New Horizons's scientific instruments collected data about Pluto's atmosphere. They studied the atmosphere's pressure and temperature. They also revealed what the atmosphere was made of. For example, one instrument detected molecules such as methane and carbon monoxide.

Another instrument watched as radio waves sent from Earth passed through Pluto's atmosphere. This was a big achievement. In the past, spacecraft could only broadcast radio signals, which would then be detected by instruments on Earth. But *New Horizons* picked up signals that were sent from Earth. This new experiment allowed the spacecraft to measure the pressure of the gas in Pluto's atmosphere.

A third instrument measured how quickly gases in the atmosphere evaporated and escaped into space. It also looked at how the sun's radiation affects Pluto.

THINK ABOUT IT ◁

Why do you think scientists might want to compare Pluto's atmosphere with Earth's atmosphere?

CHAPTER 5

PLUTO'S MOONS

Five moons orbit Pluto. The largest moon is named Charon. It is approximately half as wide as Pluto. The other moons are much smaller. Each one is less than 30 miles (48 km) wide. Scientists found those four tiny moons using the Hubble Space Telescope. They expected to find more moons once the *New Horizons* spacecraft arrived at Pluto. However, the probe discovered no new moons.

The Hubble Space Telescope photographed Pluto, Charon, and two smaller moons in 2005.

The four little moons were too small for the probe's cameras to see in detail. Still, scientists measured the moons' sizes. They also measured how bright the moons are. By combining data about each moon's size and brightness, scientists could guess how dense the moon is. They counted craters on each moon's surface to estimate how old the moon might be. Scientists think these moons have a lot of water ice on their surfaces.

Because Charon is much bigger than Pluto's other moons, the spacecraft's cameras could make out more details on its surface. Photos showed a deep canyon stretching across the moon's full width. Scientists think this canyon is 1,100 miles (1,800 km) long. It may be 4.5 miles (7.5 km) deep.

Cliffs and ridges stretch hundreds of miles across Charon's surface. Areas of the surface

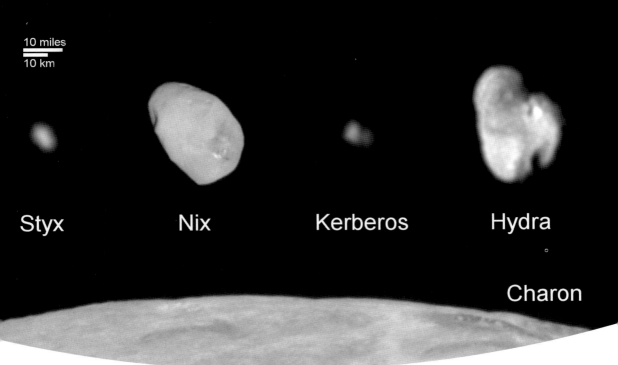

Styx   Nix   Kerberos   Hydra

Charon

▲ Unlike Charon, which is round, Pluto's four small moons are oddly shaped.

appear to have pulled apart. Because of these fractures, scientists suspect Charon might have had an underground ocean sometime in the past. They think this ocean might have frozen. As it froze, the water would have expanded. It would have stretched Charon's surface above the ice. As those areas of land stretched, they would have split apart, forming cliffs and ridges.

Other parts of Charon's surface have no craters. Some scientists even speculate that water in Charon's underground ocean might have been connected to a cryovolcano. This kind of volcano oozes slushy ice instead of hot lava. Slush from this volcano could have come to the moon's surface and filled the craters. The slush would have frozen, making the area appear smooth.

Images of Charon also show a large red patch near its northern pole. This red patch puzzled scientists at first. Then they learned what caused it. Pluto and Charon are approximately 12,200 miles (19,640 km) apart. This is much

➤ THINK ABOUT IT

Why do you think scientists search for ice on other planets and moons?

△ Charon is 754 miles (1,214 km) in diameter.

closer than Earth is to its moon. Charon is so close that it steals gases that escape from Pluto's atmosphere. Some of these gases are trapped as ice at Charon's cold north pole. When **ultraviolet** sunlight hits the ice, it causes a chemical reaction that turns the ice red.

CHAPTER 6

THE NEXT TARGET

After its historic encounter with Pluto, the *New Horizons* spacecraft continued on into the Kuiper Belt. This ring-shaped region of outer space stretches 30 to 50 times Earth's distance from the sun. Pluto is the largest known object in the Kuiper Belt. But scientists have discovered more than 1,000 other objects in this region. These objects are all cold, icy, and rocky. Some are nearly as big as Pluto.

After passing Pluto, *New Horizons* continued to fly through the Kuiper Belt.

Scientists always planned for *New Horizons* to visit at least one more object after flying by Pluto. They wanted the probe to use its scientific

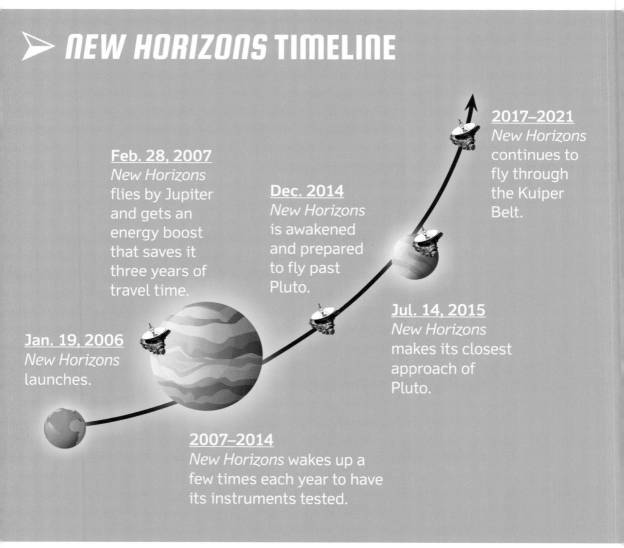

➤ *NEW HORIZONS* TIMELINE

Feb. 28, 2007
New Horizons flies by Jupiter and gets an energy boost that saves it three years of travel time.

Dec. 2014
New Horizons is awakened and prepared to fly past Pluto.

2017–2021
New Horizons continues to fly through the Kuiper Belt.

Jan. 19, 2006
New Horizons launches.

Jul. 14, 2015
New Horizons makes its closest approach of Pluto.

2007–2014
New Horizons wakes up a few times each year to have its instruments tested.

instruments to study another Kuiper Belt object. Like it did for Pluto, *New Horizons* would take pictures of the object and map its chemical content. Scientists could try to determine if the object had moons or rings. They could learn about the region around the object as well.

But when *New Horizons* launched, scientists did not know which object the probe would study. The spacecraft did not have enough fuel to change its course drastically. For this reason, scientists needed to find another object in the Kuiper Belt that would be near the spacecraft's flight path after it passed Pluto.

In 2014, scientists found an object that would work well. Known as 2014 MU69, the object is approximately 1 billion miles (1.6 billion km) beyond Pluto. Despite this distance, the probe would not need to shift its path much to reach it.

An artist's idea of what 2014 MU69 might look like

In October and November 2015, scientists sent commands to *New Horizons*. The spacecraft burned a bit of fuel four times to push itself slightly sideways. Doing so changed the probe's course just enough to pass near this new target.

However, 2014 MU69 is not the only object scientists planned to study. As *New Horizons* travels through the Kuiper Belt, it could look at 20 more objects. In 2017, the spacecraft looked at six of these objects. It sent images of them back to Earth.

Scientists are studying several aspects of these Kuiper Belt objects. They are learning about the objects' shapes and finding out how much light their surfaces reflect. As *New Horizons* continues to zoom through space, scientists will learn even more about this outer region of our solar system.

BACK TO PLUTO?

The New Horizons mission was still going on when scientists began thinking about another mission to Pluto. In April 2017, scientists met to brainstorm ideas. Researchers discussed whether they would want to orbit Pluto or focus on other objects in the Kuiper Belt.

To go into orbit, a spacecraft would have to lose energy as it neared Pluto. But Pluto's **gravity** alone is too weak to slow a spacecraft enough.

Gravity on Pluto's surface is one-sixteenth as strong as gravity on Earth's surface.

Instead, the spacecraft would need to use a rocket to slow itself down. The spacecraft would have to carry this extra rocket all the way to Pluto. It would need to bring extra fuel, too. Once the spacecraft reached Pluto, the rocket would use this extra fuel. Firing the rocket many times would keep the spacecraft from shooting past Pluto. Then the spacecraft could go into orbit.

Scientists have used a similar pattern when exploring other planets. They often begin with a flyby. Decades may pass between this first visit and an **orbiter** mission. For example, Saturn had

➤ THINK ABOUT IT

From first idea to flyby, the New Horizons mission took more than 25 years. Do you think the next mission to Pluto will take as long? Why or why not?

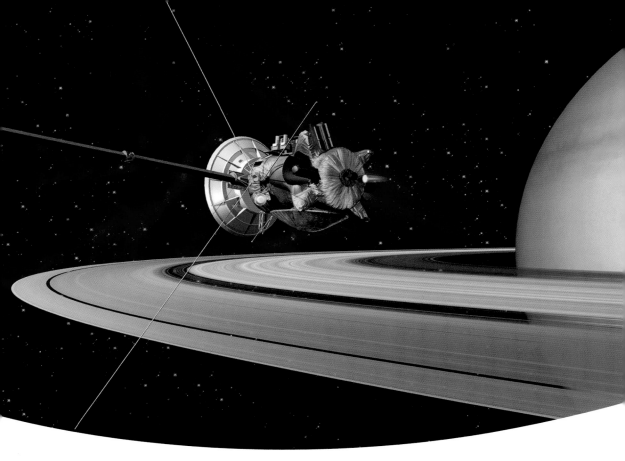

▲ *Cassini* traveled 2.2 billion miles (3.5 billion km) after its launch on October 15, 1997, to reach Saturn.

its first flyby mission in 1979. An orbiter did not arrive at the planet until 2004.

Scientists are only beginning to think of what another mission to Pluto might look like. But many people are excited to continue learning about this fascinating dwarf planet.

FOCUS ON
VOYAGE TO PLUTO

Write your answers on a separate piece of paper.

1. Write a letter to a friend about the biggest discovery that *New Horizons* made about Pluto.

2. Do you think scientists should send another spacecraft to Pluto or explore other Kuiper Belt objects instead? Why?

3. When did *New Horizons* reach Pluto?
    A. 1989
    B. 2001
    C. 2015

4. Why do scientists believe the smooth, icy areas on Pluto's surface are relatively young?
    A. They would expect older ice to be covered in craters from asteroid crashes.
    B. They would expect newer ice to be filled with particles from Pluto's atmosphere.
    C. They would expect the smooth ice to melt before it got very old.

Answer key on page 48.

GLOSSARY

antenna
A device for receiving and sending radio waves.

aperture
The opening in a camera's lens that controls how much light is let into the camera.

asteroid
A chunk of rock moving through space in orbit around the sun.

atmosphere
The layers of gases that surround a planet or moon.

craters
Round or nearly-round holes in the surface of a planet or moon, often caused by asteroid or comet crashes.

gravity
The attractive force between two objects that is due to their masses and affected by how far apart they are.

infrared
Light that is invisible to human eyes but can be seen by certain cameras and has a longer wavelength than that of visible light.

orbiter
A spacecraft that orbits a planet or moon but does not land on its surface.

probe
A device used to explore.

ultraviolet
Light that is invisible to human eyes and has a shorter wavelength than that of visible light.

TO LEARN MORE

BOOKS

Bow, James. *New Horizons: A Robot Explores Pluto and the Kuiper Belt*. New York: PowerKids Press, 2017.

Carson, Mary Kay. *Mission to Pluto: The First Visit to an Ice Dwarf and the Kuiper Belt*. Boston: Houghton Mifflin Harcourt, 2016.

Kruesi, Liz. *Space Exploration*. Minneapolis: Abdo Publishing, 2016.

Roland, James. *Pluto: A Space Discovery Guide*. Minneapolis: Lerner Publications, 2017.

NOTE TO EDUCATORS

Visit **www.focusreaders.com** to find lesson plans, activities, links, and other resources related to this title.

INDEX

2014 MU69, 39–41

asteroids, 15, 23
atmosphere, 15–16, 27–29, 35

cameras, 8, 14–15, 24–25, 32
Charon, 31–35
closest approach, 20
craters, 23, 32, 34

flyby, 15, 44–45

Jupiter, 6, 15–17

Kuiper Belt, 37–39, 41, 43

moons, 15–16, 31–35, 39

orbiter, 44–45

rocket, 8, 13, 19, 44

Saturn, 6, 44–45
scientific instruments, 13–16, 28
Stern, Alan, 10–11
surface, 20–23, 32–34, 41

water, 23, 32–34

Answer Key: **1.** Answers will vary; **2.** Answers will vary; **3.** C; **4.** A